Darrell

99

NASCAR RACING
BEHIND THE SCENES

William Burt

Lowe & B. Hould
Publishers

To Mom and Dad, Thanks!

This edition published in 1998 by
Lowe & B. Hould Publishers, an imprint of Borders, Inc.,
515 East Liberty, Ann Arbor, MI 48104.
Lowe & B. Hould Publishers is a trademark of Borders Properties, Inc.

This edition first published in 1997 by MBI Publishing Company, 729 Prospect Avenue, PO Box 1, Osceola, WI 54020-0001 USA

Library of Congress Cataloging-in-Publication Data Available

ISBN 0-681-07554-6

On the front cover: Mechanics work against the clock to get the #94 McDonald's Ford car, driven by Bill Elliott, ready for an upcoming race.

On the frontispiece: Though called a stock car, these Winston Cup cars bare little resemblance to the production cars which roll off the assembly lines. This is particularly true of the interior of the cars.—*Bill Burt*

On the title page: NASCAR racing is a sport full of color—colorful cars, colorful racewear, and plenty of colorful personalities!—*Bill Burt*

On the back cover: Winning isn't just the driver's job. The teamwork of the crew in the pits can sometimes win or lose the entire race—*Bill Burt*

Printed in Hong Kong

Contents

Goodwrench
3
Goodwrench Service
GM
oodwrench
Service
AIRBORNE

Introduction

The history of NASCAR is filled with ex-moonshiners, mechanics, farmer's sons and others who had one thing in common. They loved cars, wanted to go fast, and they thrived on competition. The dirt tracks and early asphalt tracks did, and still do, give the average racer an opportunity to go fast and test his skill against other average racers. But NASCAR grew from two things: the above average racers who could consistently drive on the edge and not fall off, and the fans who would come out to see them race. Only money from the fans could allow the drivers and crews to race as a full-time career. And as the cream of the drivers rose to the top, so did the events. The best could draw the big crowds. Tracks became bigger and better, both for the drivers and fans. The sport began to build on itself. Better drivers, bigger purses and more exposure. The fan base began to grow. Soon there was an opportunity for someone to pull it all together. So began the National Association of Stockcar Automobile Racing.

People still come to the track or turn on the television to see the best drivers race. As a result, racing has produced a lot of millionaires. Over the last twenty years the sport has exploded in growth, and as Winston Cup racing heads into the twenty-first century, it is changing at a great pace. New speedways, new races, more and more sponsorship and multi-car teams all are coming into play and are slowly changing the sport. As a result, short track races are in jeopardy. The tracks have too few seats to offer the purses that larger tracks offer. And restricter plate racing has dramatically changed the races at Daytona and Talladega. Also, the advent of the multi-car teams threatens to drastically change the sport. Many fear that the one-car teams will never be able to keep up, able to do only a portion of testing that the multi-car teams do. Money has always been important in racing, but it is more important now than it has ever been. Things have certainly changed, but there are still two constants: drivers who want to go fast, and people who want to watch them.

Goodwrench
3
Havoline
28
98
9

Driving the Course

CHAPTER 1

The day has finally ended and work is over. You hop in your Mustang or Chevy pick-up. In your mind your crew is giving last minute instructions. You wink at your arch rival who starts on the outside of row one. You're on the pole. (I always am.) You fire the motor, check the gauges, ease out of the parking lot. The guard at the front gate is in his Winston Cup official uniform, and he waves you onto the road. The first traffic light turns from red to green. Green flag! You nail it and the race begins.

Bobby Allison said one reason that Winston Cup has become so popular is that the fans can relate to driving in a Winston Cup race. They drive a car that looks much like a racecar every day and can easily see themselves behind the wheel of a Winston Cup car.

Superspeedways

Racers face many different driving tasks throughout the year, starting with a superspeedway race at Daytona. Superspeedways are tracks two miles and up and can be broken into two groups: restricter plate tracks and non-restricter plate tracks.

Driving at Daytona and Talladega (the only two restricter plate tracks) has dramatically changed with the

Nose to tail at 200 miles per hour. Unlike many lightweight racecars Winston Cup cars weigh in at 3,600 pounds.

From half mile short tracks to over two and half mile superspeedways, each week drivers see a different look from the track.

advent of the restricter plate. Cars now stay bunched up on the track, nose to tail, using the other car's draft. With restricter plates, drafting is not an option; it's the only option.

The car in front breaks through the air and if the second car is close enough, this car will get in the slipstream of the first car and will not have to break through the air. This decreases the air resistance on the front of the car and allows it to go faster. The first car also benefits from this. The car behind "cleans up" the air coming off the back of the first car. Instead of falling off the back of the first car and becoming turbulent, the air flows more smoothly off the first car's rear spoiler and onto the hood of the back car. This cleaner air flow allows the first car more speed.

When passing at Talladega or Daytona, a driver can't rely on raw horsepower as much as at other tracks. The restricter plate has taken away most of the throttle response and it takes a while for the motor to come up to speed. Thus begins a cat and mouse game of who drafts with whom. A Ford will probably have a better chance of getting drafting help from another Ford than a Chevy. However, on the last lap of the Daytona 500 a driver will draft behind anything going fast enough to help him. Buddy Baker once said that on the track a driver can count his friends on his thumb. Nowhere is this more evident than on the track at Talladega and Daytona.

With restricter plates the driver never gets off of the throttle. If he does, the car will lose positions, since it takes a long time to "wind back up" a restricter plate motor. If he has to slow a little, a driver will apply the brake lightly with the left foot while keeping the car at full throttle with the right. A car's success at a restricter

Three wide is common on many tracks. It's usually a good idea to get down to at least two wide and on some tracks it's a mandatory rule to go only one wide.

plate track will be based on a driver's ability to draft.

Friends are made on one lap and lost on the next. Any driver will leave another hung out to dry. A car cannot run alone and survive. As a result of this nose-to-tail drafting, drivers must endure 500 miles of super-attentive driving. With the high speeds and tight packs of cars, a small mistake that a driver could get away with at another track may take out half the cars in the field at a restricter plate track.

Other little problems must also be anticipated. If a driver tucks up closely behind another car, the decreased

Rusty Wallace, 1989 Winston Cup Champion is a master of the short tracks.

air resistance will take some strain off the motor and allow it to rev up more. If the motor is already redlined this may blow it up. Drivers must anticipate these dangers and counter with a tap of the brake.

Other shorter superspeedways such as Michigan are run without restricter plates. On these tracks drivers don't have to rely on someone else's car to stay up front. Often the track has two "grooves," meaning there is more than one line that a driver can take and still get around the track fast. This usually means that a driver can take a low line or a high line. The low line is the shortest way around the track, as the driver is going around a smaller circle. The high line is the longer way around, but because the radius of the turn is not as tight, the driver can keep the motor wound up and it may be possible to carry more speed through the turn. This allows the driver to carry more speed coming out of the turn, and as the cars begin the drag race down the straightaway, the driver will have an advantage.

Other tracks, such as Indianapolis, are one groove tracks. There is only one fast line through the turn, and track position is critical. Mistakes on the track that allow other cars to pass become costly. Even if a car is faster, it will be difficult to repass the slower cars, and in doing so, the driver may "use up " his tires. The harder to pass on the track, the more important it is to pass during pit stops. On these tracks, cars may take only two tires during a pit stop, favoring track position over the "fresh tire" advantage.

Intermediate Tracks

The next step down from the superspeedways are the intermediate tracks, such as Dover or Atlanta, which range from one to two miles. Many of these tracks are also two groove tracks. With lower speeds, slight contact between the cars becomes more common and driving style and rhythm become critical.

When racing, smooth is fast. A 'herky-jerky' driving style may be fast on a lap or two here and there, but consistent speed comes from smooth driving and patience—taking care of the car. Tire condition becomes more and more critical. Worn tires will slow a car down as much as dragging an anchor.

The exhaust exits in front of the rear tires. Some teams run it out both sides and some just the left to keep the pipes from being pinched shut as the car rolls in the turns.

Short Tracks

After intermediate tracks come the short tracks. With track size half or three quarters of a mile, short track racing is vastly different from other types of tracks. The laps are fast. At Bristol, a half-mile track, the lap time is a little over fifteen seconds. At this pace, losing a half a second a lap to the leader of the race means going a lap down in thirty laps. But losing a lap does not mean that it can't be overcome. During a restart, the lapped cars line up in the inside with the cars on the lead lap on the outside. If a lapped driver can get ahead of the leader of the race and catch a caution flag, he will go to the back of the outside line on the next restart and will be back on the lead lap. This can be a tricky situation for a driver, because if he's a lap down, his car is probably not as fast as the leader's. But by starting on the inside the driver has superior track position. If he can just stay out front for a few laps, he might get lucky. It has been done many times and many drivers have gone on to win races after being one or more lap down.

On a short track, it's every man for himself. If a car is holding up someone behind him, the driver can probably expect a little tap from behind to let him know he's in the way. This type of racing may get you a penalty at Talladega, but it really won't get a second look at Martinsville. The theory is that if the lead car was fast enough to get its rear bumper out of the way, it wouldn't be there when the other driver's front bumper came along. If a car gets its nose inside another car's it has the preferred position. If the car is on the inside it may "lean on" the outside car; after all, eight tires handle better than four.

Driving a short track puts demands on a racecar. The driver is on and off the throttle, either accelerating or decelerating. Also, more demand is put on the brakes. If they are abused, they will overheat and lose much of their efficiency.

Road Courses

Finally there are the road courses, Sears Point and Watkins Glen. These tracks throw a real curve at the drivers and teams. All of a sudden the cars have to turn right as well as left. Drivers shift more, brake more, and turn more than at any other type of track. There is one fastest way around a road course and the best way to pass is when the car ahead makes a mistake and deviates from its line.

Road courses are the only places where it's good to be in the pits when the caution comes out. On all other tracks, it usually means going a lap down. On a road course, it means a driver can stay out during the caution while the other cars pit, and be leading on the restart.

24
DUPONT
24
AUTOMOTIVE FINISHES
DUPONT
GMAC
Goodwrench
Service
3

Building a Team

CHAPTER 2

You're in the front yard waxing your Trans Am or Mercedes. They broadcast the winning lottery numbers over the radio. You can't believe it. You've hit the lottery and have the millions that you always dreamed of. Maybe driving isn't your bag, but racing is. It's time to do what you've always wanted—quit your job and buy your own Winston Cup car.

During the race, Winston Cup is all driving, racing, fast pit stops, strategy, cool uniforms, trucks—the whole bit. But the proposition of owning and running a race car is all business. It's also a lot of hard work. While the car styles are common and much of the design (push rod V-8s, solid rear axles) is low tech stuff compared to Formula 1 or Indy Cars, the plan to refine more and more speed out of the low tech stuff is just as, if not more, difficult, and very expensive.

Two of the hottest competitors on the circuit—Dale Earnhardt, the consummate veteran driver and Jeff Gordon, the leader of the next generation of drivers. Earnhardt has seven Winston Cup Championships and Gordon won his first in 1995.

Sponsorship

The first thing it takes to win or even make the race is money—lots of money. If you see a car winning, you can bet that there's a deep pocket behind it. Sponsors pay from about three to seven million dollars a year to run a Cup car. Usually the more money spent, the better the chance of winning. Big bucks mean more people, more cars, more motors and most importantly, more testing, not only at the track (it's limited by NASCAR) but also in-house. Big budgets mean you can tear some things up while experimenting. (And whether you are testing cars or space shuttles, improvements are made because of failures. Where would our space program be today, if we hadn't blown up so many rockets in the 1950s figuring out how to make one work?) A team can only find the maximum specs on a motor by going past the maximum, and blowing the motor up. Once you find that point, you can back up just a hair and know you're maxed out. If you don't have the money to blow things up, it's hard to know if you're leaving some horsepower in the shop.

Even with the big budgets, racing is still a deal for a sponsor. For the advertising money that can buy a few ads during the Superbowl, a company can sponsor a NASCAR race team for an entire season. It gives a company the opportunity to associate itself with fast-paced action and all of the thrills of racing. Many a business deal has been smoothed over by taking a client to the pits on raceday at Daytona.

However, a team has to find a sponsor. The best chance of landing a sponsor is to run well, yet it's hard to run well without a sponsor. A new or unsponsored team must have the funds to run well while courting a potential sponsor. When a team runs without a sponsor, it's a game of time. They must land the sponsor before they run out of money. With a set of tires costing $1,300.00, and an engine $30,000-$50,000, it's hard to last long. Alan Kulwicki didn't have a sponsor, not too long before he became Winston Cup Champion.

In modern racing, a driver's job goes well beyond just driving the car. Sponsors finance racing programs and in return market their products through racing. Drivers become spokespersons for the sponsoring companies. Many times these turn into long term business relationships. Few people can pick up a can of STP without thinking of Richard Petty. Drivers lead a hectic life not only at

Dale Earnhardt and Richard Childress have combined to create a modern Winston Cup Legend.

the track, but also for the sponsor. They make personal appearances, attend autograph signings, and show up for other company functions, allowing the sponsor to get the most from their investment in a racing program. As drivers often become spokespeople for the company, they must make sure that their actions and comments are acceptable to the sponsor.

Once you have the money, you have to know how to spend it. It takes many components to build a successful racing program. The shop, the people and the racecars are the foundation of the effort.

The Shop

The shop is the first order of business. It must be spacious and crammed full of expensive equipment. It must be part assembly shop, part machine shop and part garage. Painting facilities, cleaning facilities, a dynamometer room, parts storage and preparation areas, and offices must be built, bought, or rented. Some shops even have weight rooms, museums and souvenir shops. Setting up a well-equipped shop can easily cost into the millions. Once the shop is complete, it's time to start hiring.

The Chevrolet Monte Carlo was reintroduced in 1995 and has had great success.

The Team

Racing is a team sport. A real race fan pulls for the team, not just for the driver. People in racing seldom say, "Earnhardt's running well," they say, "The number 3 car is running well." Usually a driver's first comment after winning a race is, "I gotta thank the crew and the guys at the shop for giving me a great car." A great driver is a wonderful team member, just as a great quarterback is. And the success of the car is based on the team as a whole.

The driver, crew chief, engine builder, team manager, body fabricators, general mechanics, public relations managers, and other specialists must be hired. The mix of the team is very important. You can have geniuses in every position, but if they don't get along and work well together, they probably won't be successful. Add to this the fact that the 'Championship Team' for the last five years has averaged 25.4 losses per year (or lost over 85 percent of the time). Racing can be a damn depressing proposition. Baseball teams winning a game by 11 runs in the ninth inning don't have to worry about losing the game because all of their bats explode, but race teams do. In 1990, Dale Earnhardt would have won the Daytona 499 1/2, but a flat tire kept him from winning the Daytona 500.

Position by position, a successful race team requires excellence. A small detail overlooked when preparing the car or a miscue in the pits, may cost the team a race. Every year a few oil lines are found to be loose, driveshafts not connected, or batteries left unhooked—on the first lap of the race.

A successful crew listens to one another and remains open to change. If a team stands still in the development area, they will be going backwards. Usually the driving force coordinating this "constant improvement" is the crew chief.

Crew Chief

While the driver gets most of the spotlight during the race, the crew chief is usually the one who puts it all

The Ford Thunderbird is currently the oldest body style run on the circuit.

together. The crew chief oversees the preparation of the car and must be able to work with the driver during testing, practice and the race to "dial the car in," or constantly improve the handling set-up. The crew chief must work with the engine builder to look for an edge in gearing the car so that the most can be gotten from the engine on any given track. The crew chief must listen to every one of his team members and associates, searching for ideas that will give the edge on the track.

It's the crew chief who is responsible for the technical aspects of the racecar and the crew. This includes car preparation at the shop and at the track. Simply put, the crew chief's job is to make sure everything gets done and gets done properly. In Winston Cup racing, the buck stops with the crew chief.

Long before the season starts, the crew chief is hard at work preparing the stable of cars necessary to run a Winston Cup team. The frames and roll cages must be built or purchased. Then bodies must be put on the car. Some teams may buy cars assembled; however, many teams choose to make their own bodies. As the cars are assembled they must be tested not only on the track but also in the wind tunnel. As teams build different cars for different types of tracks (speedways, short tracks and road courses), crew chiefs must be able to understand the variety of tracks, help to build cars for every category, as well as refine a particular car for a particular track.

Engine Specialist

The engine specialist is responsible for the preparation of the engines at the shop, during practice and qualifying, and during the race. The engine specialist is also responsible for rebuilding the engines between races. A number of engines will be prepared at the shop before heading out to the track. These engines will have been run on the dyno to ensure that they are building enough power and that the power comes on in the right rpm range for the track on which they will race. When the teams swap engines at the track, the new engine is usually ready to be run immediately. This advanced engine

The Pontiac Grand Prix. Its body was updated for 1996.

preparation is what makes it possible for teams to blow an engine at the end of practice Saturday and still be able to race competitively on Sunday with an engine that has not yet been run on the track.

Engine builders must evaluate similar components and decide which is best to use. Many hours of testing and retesting are required to make a sound decision. Engine builders must constantly look for the small changes that can be made to gain a quarter of a horsepower here and half a horsepower there. The more of these small "tricks" that an engine builder knows, the bigger an advantage the driver will have at the track.

Fabricator

Fabricators are the artists who build the bodies, and in some teams the chassis, of the cars. Most of the body of the car comes into the shop in the form of sheet metal. Fabricators size, cut, bend and fit body pieces to make the final product. Their work must be very precise, since the cars built by all of the different race teams must fit the very precise templates used for pre-race inspection.

Mechanics

Each team must have a number of good mechanics. Each week everything from carburetors to rearends must be taken apart, checked and rebuilt. All of the pieces must be prepared and then assembled for the race. Most of these mechanics have particular areas in which they specialize. Teams may have a suspension specialist who takes apart the suspension after the race, tests the parts, and replaces those that show wear or damage, rebuilding the suspension for the next race. Others may handle areas such as rear ends and axles, another cylinder heads, and still another, clutch and transmissions. By delegating the work in this way, team members can establish routines that eliminate failures at the track.

When hiring the team, it is important to keep in mind that some team members will need to pull double duty, a job at the shop and a job on the pit crew during the race.

Western Auto's
PARTS AMERICA
17
ACDelco
TOUCH ONE by
ACDelco
GOODYEAR
BUSCH
Bowman
Stant
Prestone
3M
RCA
JESEL
CRAFTSMAN
MOOG
SIMPSON
STP
Western Auto

Building the Car

CHAPTER 3

Once the team is hired, it's time to get the cars ready to race.

You are almost through building your 123rd Winston Cup car model. This collection complements your 96 diecast collectible car collection. You like dirty fingernails, detailed work and building something beautiful. When you see a show car on display in front of a grocery store, those little hairs on the back of your neck stand up and your heart beats a little faster. You may not know it, but you are an untrained Winston Cup car builder.

A modern Winston Cup team will prepare many cars in order to run a full season. A short track car run at Martinsville or Bristol wouldn't be successful at a superspeedway, such as Daytona or Talladega. Year by year, cars become specialized more and more for a particular track, especially races like the Daytona 500 and Brickyard 400 where the prestige and the purse warrant the extra expense. If a team is very successful at a particular track with a particular car, the team may set the car aside, running it only at that track or another track which

The main floor of Darrell Waltrip's shop just a few miles from Charlotte Speedway. Teams may have a dozen or so cars in various stages of construction.

The beginning of a racecar. Some teams buy these chassis and some build them in house. A steel surface plate (an expensive item) is a necessity.

is very similar. Two cars are taken to each track, a primary and a backup. If things go well and nothing happens to the primary car, the back-up car will never come off the trailer.

Some teams begin by building their own chassis. Many put their own bodies on the car. All custom fit the suspension components and drivetrain in the car. Motors must be built, tuned and tested. Once all of the parts are in the right place the real work begins.

Currently on the Winston Cup Race schedule, there are 31 points paying races run on 18 different tracks. And keep in mind that a set-up that runs well during the Daytona 500 in February may not run well at the same track in the 400 mile race in July. Through race experience, testing, practice and help from other "friendly" teams, the team must figure a way to be competitive week in and week out. Finishing "unwell" week in and week out can, putting it mildly, give the sponsor great concern.

NASCAR Specifications

The cars that race today may look somewhat like the production cars they are named after, but that's pretty much where the similarities end. Cup cars are a paradox. They are on the cutting edge of "yesterday's" technology.

Fabricators are as much artist as mechanic, handmaking much of the car's body from stock sheet metal. Years of training are required to be able to build cars from scratch.

Winston Cup cars must be built within certain specifications established by NASCAR which eliminate many of today's exotic materials and designs except for the safety systems of the car.

Technology seen in other racing venues—turbochargers, overhead cam configurations, advanced aerodynamics, in-car computer telemetry, and extensive use of materials such as carbon fiber, are not allowed in Winston Cup racing. This forces the teams to rely on better engineering of old technology and focus more attention to the race set-up.

Many times in the past, the rules have been changed to slow the cars down, requiring the engineers to continue to search for changes that give that small, but important, advantage on the track. It may take a while, but they always seem to get the speed back.

Winston Cup cars don't come down the assembly lines in Detroit, yet teams have many options open to them when it comes to car supply. The first basic component is the roll cage/chassis. Most teams buy these from various suppliers such as Hopkins, Loughlin and Hutcherson-Pagan. Recently some teams have opted to build their chassis in house. By doing so, teams are able to make small changes in the design of the car (such as the suspension geometry) that give better handling in particular situations.

The Chassis

The chassis is built from the bottom up. Assembly starts with the frame rail and proceeds upwards. Frame rails, the bottom frame components, are carbon steel tubing, built parallel with no offsets. The rocker panels and frame pieces are square tubing .120 inches thick. All of the connections that attach the frame pieces together are welded. Chassis pieces must be cut and shaped and all sharp edges deburred before being assembled.

All of the individual pieces must be fitted precisely if the finished product is to be correct. The chassis is assembled on a "jig," a permanent piece of equipment in the shop. Pieces ready to be welded are clamped onto the jig to be held in place while welding. By using this and other fixtures, the builders achieve consistency from chassis to chassis. The current trend is to build the chassis a bit differently for different types of tracks. The chassis can be different, but the teams must know where it is different.

Engine performance is recorded on the dyno. Where in the powerband the engine makes its power is very important on the track.

If there is an unknown deviation when the chassis is built, it can mean an ill-handling headache at the track. The other problem is that the chassis can work great, but unless the team pays careful attention as to how it was built, they won't know what made the car so good, nor be able to duplicate the assembly later.

The firewall, the floorpan, and the rear wheel wells are about the only sheet metal pieces added during the building of the chassis. Suspension fittings are added to the frame rails. Again, for the finished car to handle properly, all of these must be positioned correctly.

A full machine shop is a necessity. Here a cylinder head goes through final machining before assembly.

The Body

Once the chassis is bought or built, a body must be put on. Before the engine goes in and the body goes on, there is no difference between the Fords, Chevrolets or Pontiacs. What makes the car will be decided when the body is hung on the chassis. There have been many chassis that have run more than one type of body in their lifetime. Very few OEM body parts are used on a modern stockcar. Most pieces are hand crafted by the car builder. The roof panel, hood and part of the deck lid are usually the only OEM body parts used. The front facia and rear nose piece are manufactured specifically for the Winston Cup series and their shape is closely monitored by NASCAR. In fact, each bears its own serial number. The body pieces are riveted and welded onto the chassis. Once the body panels are in place, the seams are ground flush, and after minor body work, the car is primered.

Components

With the chassis and body complete the teams begin to mount suspension components, drivetrain, and outfit the cockpit with seat, gauges and safety equipment. When this is complete, all that's left to do is drop in a motor and transmission and the car is ready to go to the track. This assembly process is much harder than it sounds. At each step the car builder must make sure that what he's doing is fitting together correctly, is legal, and is safe for the driver. Some of the more recent changes in chassis construction were made only for driver safety. For instance, a fifth horizontal roll bar has been added in the door area to help protect the driver in side impacts, and a roll bar has been added in the center of the windshield so a tire or other debris encountered in a wreck won't come into the cockpit with the driver.

The Engine

Most shops build their own motors; others buy or rent them. The engine builder is limited in the number of modifications that can be made when building the engines.

All Winston Cup engines are limited to 358 cubic inches. They use iron blocks, aluminum cylinder heads, and run around 16 to 1 compression, rated at around 750 horsepower.

The engine is hooked up and run in one room and monitored from another for safety. While "meltdowns" aren't common they can be impressive when an engine does let go.

It's the same old solid lifter V-8 with a four barrel. Only small block V-8 engines are allowed. Legally you can run Chevrolet 307, 327, 350 and 400 small blocks and Ford 302 and 351 blocks. Regardless of which is used, the engine must be built to have a displacement of between 350 and 358 cubic inches. The cast iron four bolt main blocks used in Winston Cup Racing are manufactured by the race divisions of General Motors and Ford (Aluminum blocks are not allowed). They mainly differ from the production blocks in that they have thicker cylinder walls to eliminate distortion and give a better surface for the rings. Improved water passages increase the cooling ability. Adding bulkhead material to the main bearing bosses adds strength around the crankshaft. Increased strength around the deck surface where the heads bolt on increases engine stability and allows for the

Parts storage alone can take up a large part of the shop. Shock rebound and dampening can be fine tuned to many different settings, which in turn requires many shocks. Each team has a "shock dyno" to test and evaluate the shock absorber performance.

D5134
EAGLE
#1
LF-7

Piece by piece the body is attached to the car. Most pieces are hand-fabricated. Only the hood skin, roof skin and deck lid are used.

high rpms run today. Teams may not change the angle of cylinders, number and type of main bearings, or the location of the camshaft.

The "bottom end" of the motor is built for strength. Only steel crankshafts are allowed and most have been lightened and balanced. The crankshaft lobes are tapered on the leading edges to reduce windage and weight in order to increase engine response and horsepower. Winston Cup cars may use any type of piston. Most are forged aluminum of varying design. Strong H-beam style rods and high quality bearings round out the heavy duty bottom end of the motor.

Cylinder heads are aluminum. Recent changes in the rules have limited the available heads to one Ford and one General Motors head design. Valve location and angle must remain stock. Internal polishing and "porting" (custom machining the intake and exhaust ports on the cylinder head to match the manifold ports) are allowed. Before this rule, there were many more types of cylinder heads available; as they were modified more and more, a team could easily have $20,000 to $30,000 in a set of heads.

The Cup cars run very radical cams for flat tappet lifters. The lobe designs of General Motors and Ford camshafts are similar, with slight differences between the two. The Ford camshaft is shorter and thicker, an inherently stronger design than the GM camshafts which are longer and narrower.

The valve train is pretty straightforward and of the highest quality. Lifters are solid steel. Pushrods are a high quality racing type, able to withstand the tremendous force within the valve train. Most teams use roller bearing rocker arms of a "split shaft" design which are much stronger than production rocker arms. Valve springs are made from a high quality steel. As engine speeds have increased, all valve train components have become difficult parts to manufacture. Winston Cup engine speeds have increased to the point where turning over 9,000rpm is common.

Most teams buy the rollcage/chassis. A few teams build them in house which allows for more control and experimentation.

The unpolished finished product. Much cosmetic bodywork must be done before going to the track.

Fuel System

The fuel system is old technology. Winston Cup cars run four-barrel, mechanically advanced, secondary venturi carburetors. Some polishing and other minor internal changes are allowed, but no external alterations are made. Carburetor jets must be the same type as supplied by the manufacturer.

Carburetors are inspected closely by racing officials. At Talladega and Daytona restricter plates, mounted between the carburetor and the intake manifold, are used to limit the amount of fuel/air vapor to the engine. The result is less air, lower RPMs, less horsepower and lower speeds. High performance, aluminum intake manifolds are used, provided they are models that have been approved by NASCAR officials.

Winston Cup cars are required to use a fuel cell with a steel body and an internal bladder that is much stronger than a stock tank and much harder to damage. They are partitioned so that in the event of a rupture, the fuel will not gush out of the opening.

Intake manifold modifications can make the same engine run very differently. Epoxy fillers may be added to

MONTE CARLO
GOODYEAR
plasti-kote
STP
SIMPSON
MOOG
BUSCH
10

Cleanliness is next to godliness when building motors. Building areas look more like laboratories than garages.

This Monte Carlo is ready to finish. Once all the body work is done, the suspension and cockpit are completed. Then add paint and a motor and it's ready to go to the track.

the individual runners to change the flow characteristics of the manifold. Fillers may not be added to the plenum floor or walls. This "manifold tuning" has become an art in itself. All Winston Cup cars use a round, dry-type air filter, much the same as the one used on production vehicles.

Exhaust System

The exhaust system is made up of three main components: the headers, the collector pipe and the exhaust pipes. These can be configured differently (changing their shape and length) to further tune the powerband of the motor. Exhaust pipes exit the car at the side between the front and rear wheels. They may exit the car on either side. Some teams locate both pipes on the left side of the car. This eliminates the chance that they might be "pinched" shut as the car pitches over in the turns.

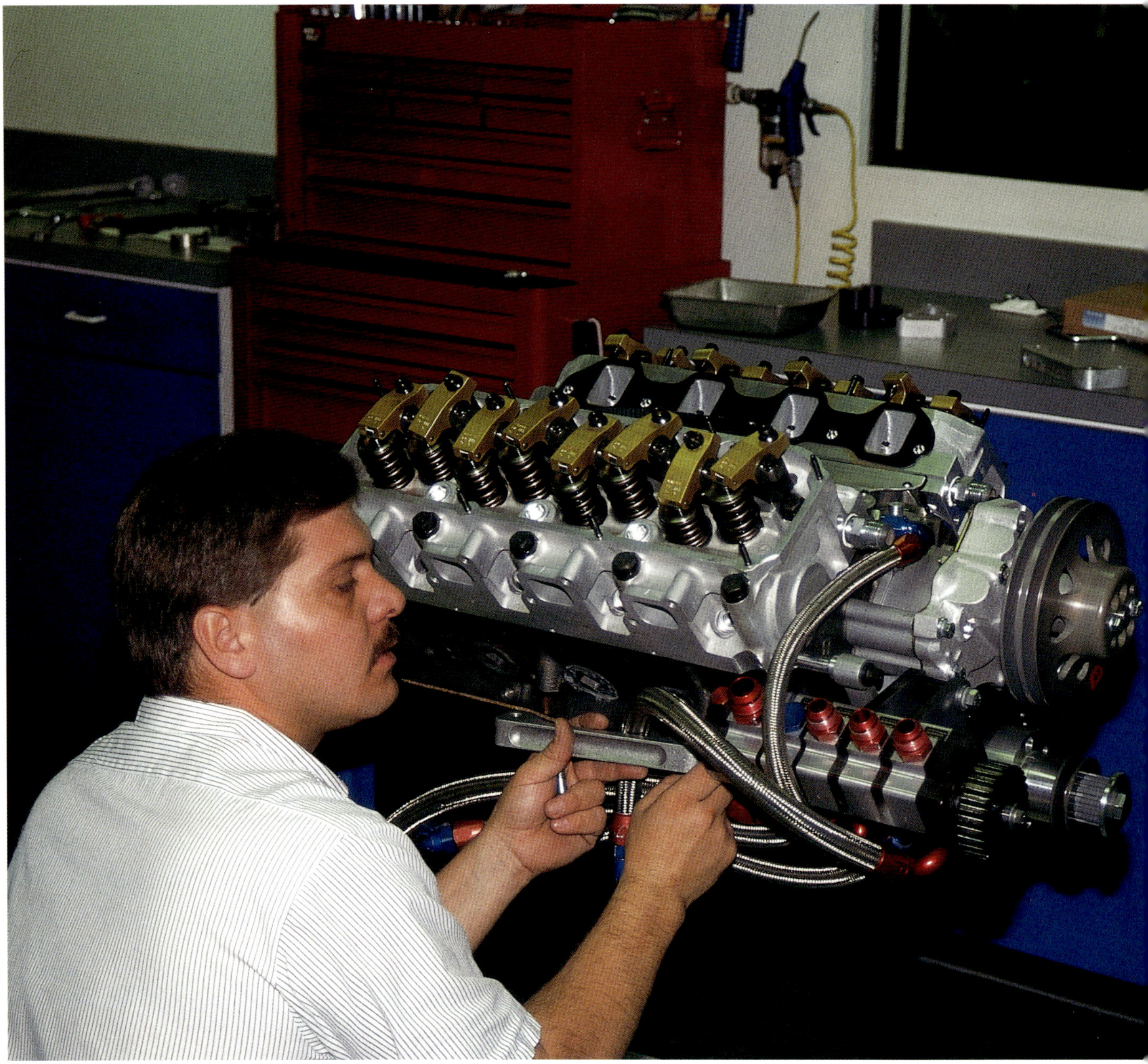

With a design that is strictly limited by NASCAR, engine builders are still able to crank out over 700 horsepower.

Tuning is done at the shop. Teams will take five or six motors to the track and all of them must be ready to go at a moment's notice.

Oil System

The oil system on a Winston Cup car varies greatly from production oil systems. Cup cars use a "dry sump" oil system. Instead of the oil flowing down to the pan to be recycled through the engine by a pump that picks up the oil from the bottom of the oil pan, the dry sump systems keep the oil in motion at all times. The pump is mounted on the outside of the engine (much the same as an alternator is mounted) and is driven by a belt. After the oil runs through the engine, it is quickly "picked up" and pumped through the oil system. During circulation, the oil passes through many feet of hose, an oil reservoir tank mounted in the left rear of the car, and an oil cooler mounted in the left front of the car. The oil cooler is a fairly vulnerable piece of equipment. Often a Winston Cup car cannot survive impact to the left front that might be survivable to the right front because of the oil cooler. The system holds around 18 quarts of oil, runs at about 70 to 80 p.s.i. and maintains an acceptable range of oil temperature from 250 to 270 degrees F.

Great attention is paid to every component of the engine during assembly.

Ignition System

For ignition, high quality after-market distributors and plug wires are used. Electronic ignition systems fire the system, but no computerized systems are allowed. The major ignition system components are located in the cockpit, to the right of the driver. This protects the equipment from debris and heat. Two separate ignition systems are in the car. In the event of an ignition failure, the driver can quickly flip a switch, changing to the back-up system without having to make a pit stop.

From crankshaft to valves, engine builders are limited by their weakest link. This link changes as engines continue to develop. At one time, valve springs were failing far too often. Engine builders demanded a better product from their suppliers and the suppliers responded. But by making the springs stronger, this allowed the engine builders to push for more power which will uncover the next weakest link in the motor.

Now that the cars are built, it's time to head to the track and try to make them go fast.

Cooling System

Winston cup cooling systems are also similar to their production counterparts but with a few modifications. With the compression ratios being run and the high engine speeds being turned, much more heat is generated than in a production engine. Only high strength hoses are used in the cooling system, with the lower radiator hose most often being a one-piece, metal pipe. Other hoses are braided stainless steel with special high pressure fittings. Radiators are aluminum, stock appearing and mounted in the stock position. Screens help prevent debris from entering the radiator. A modified water pump gives more output than a stock pump can provide. All fans (electric) must have a diameter of at least 14 inches.

Top Right
Grill openings are very important to Winston Cup cars. Not only do they supply cool air to the radiator, but also to the brakes. They may be taped over to eliminate drag and front end lift.

Bottom Right
A great deal of attention is paid to the rear spoiler. A higher angle means more downforce for better handling in the turns, but also means more drag down the straight aways. Support rods keep the spoiler from laying down at speed.

Pilot
ESTABLISHED 1904
Badcock
HOME FURNISHING CENTERS
12
Mane 'n Tail
Ford
KLINGSPOR
Abrasives
EARL'S
PERFORMANCE PRODUCTS
Mighty
ENGINE
GUARD
FILTERS

Western Auto
QUICKCAR
17 DARRELL WALTRIP
www.dw17.com
Western Auto's
PARTS AMERICA

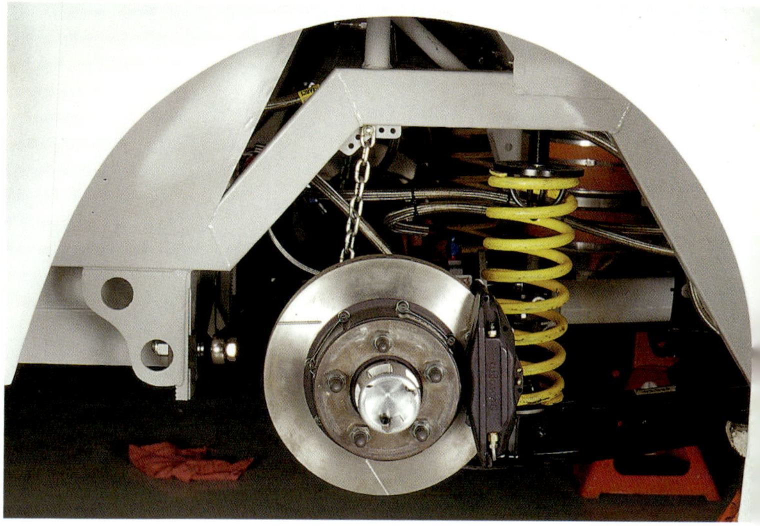

Wedge adjustments increase spring pressure. By tightening the bolt, the spring is tightened, and its spring rate is increased.

The driver's office. Safety items include a fire extinguishing system, padded roll bars and shock resistant seat. Gauges are large and easy to see. The primary and secondary ignition systems are mounted to the right of the driver.

Little
Raybestos
15

Track Time

CHAPTER 4

You're under your 1972 Corvette changing the rear end oil. As you squeeze more in, you lay your head back into the pan of old ninety weight oil. You cuss and bitch and moan and try to clean up. Your friend thinks something is terribly wrong, and doesn't understand how you consider this type of work fun. The smell of the burnt oil in your hair does not bother you as much as that little flutter in the motor at 4,000rpm. Instead of a paint job, you buy more suspension and motor. Yes, with a lifetime of training you are ready to be a successful Winston Cup crew chief.

Together the driver and the crew chief make the car go fast. The driver drives and the crew chief organizes the team effort under hectic circumstances.

Race Week

The travel schedule for crews is intense. With thirty-two races (the Daytona 500 taking 2 weeks in itself), testing sessions, and other miscellaneous travel, crew members and drivers spend much of their year on the road. Day by day and week by week, the crew chief and the team repeat a hectic routine.

During "happy hour," the last practice before the race, track time is essential. It's the last time the car will be on the track until the race.

Driver/owner Ricky Rudd keeps an eye on the competition from the top of his car hauler during practice.

Monday. Work begins as the trailer is unloaded from the previous Sunday's race. Truck drivers usually head out from the track immediately after the race, sometimes running all night in order to get the rig and equipment back to the shop as soon as possible. Once the rig is back at the shop, all of the race gear must be unloaded, checked, and, if necessary, cleaned, rebuilt, replaced, or repaired. The rig itself is cleaned and serviced, making it ready to head out for the next race.

Tuesday & Wednesday. Depending on the outcome of the previous race, the work load differs. If the car managed to make it through the race undamaged, it may only need cosmetic work to prepare it for the next time it is to be raced. Cars that have been damaged must be fixed. These repairs can range from relatively minor sheet metal work to major surgery requiring large sections to be repaired or replaced. If a car is totaled, it must be replaced with a new car. Teams may have many racecars available at any one time, and it is not usually necessary to race the same car two weeks in a row. The team concentrates on preparing the car for the next race, but if a damaged car is to be raced in the future, time must be found for repairs.

The primary and backup cars and engines for the next race must be made ready. All the systems in the cars must be set up, checked and rechecked. Qualifying, race and backup engines must be built and tested on the dyno.

Once all of these preparations are completed, the rig must be restocked and inventoried to ensure that the team will have everything they will need at the track.

Thursday. The rig and team must be ready to head out so that they can reach their destination the day before qualifying. In recent years the three-day race weekend has become popular, giving the teams more time to prepare cars and also giving them more time at home, a critical factor with thirty-one races in the year. Six to eight people may be enough to get the car through qualifying and practice, but on race day twelve to twenty people will be nec-

Rousch Racing's Mark Martin and Bobby Allison Motorsport's crew chief Jimmy Fennig discuss handling during a break at the track.

Sterling Marlin takes a time-out with the competition. Many friendships in racing extend past the boundaries of the teams.

essary to take care of all the jobs. Most teams bring people to the race only as they are needed, with the full race team not being assembled until late Saturday or early Sunday.

It is the crew chief's job to coordinate their efforts. The action at the track during the race weekend is tightly scheduled by NASCAR and much has to be done quickly.

Friday. At about 6:00 A.M. the trucks come into the track. The trucks are parked and garage location decided by a team's position in the points. If there are more cars trying to qualify than garage stalls, somebody must work outside. As soon as the trucks are parked, the unloading begins—the car, tool boxes, tire racks, more tool boxes, air tanks, generators, everything from coolers to banners.

Geoff Bodine living the tough life of a race driver.

The constant worries of the crew chief. Ray Everham now produces arguably the best prepared racecar week in and week out.

With more wins than any active driver (84), Darrell Waltrip prepares to qualify.

Before first light the haulers are usually lined up at the garage gate.

As the rig is emptied of equipment, it becomes the base of operation for the weekend.

The qualifying set-up is the first order of business. On a qualifying run, the car starts from a dead stop from pit road, builds up speed around the track, takes the green flag at the start/finish line, runs two fast laps, then shuts it off. The chassis set-up that works well on long runs is no good here. Tires handle better when they have been warmed up by running a few laps. However, on a qualifying run, the set-up must be good just as the tires are warming up. Track time (for practice) before qualifying is limited. What's available is filled with quick trips from the track and back to the garage. The driver runs a couple of laps, and the crew chief usually climbs up and watches from the top of the trailer. Together they try to dial in the suspension, which means getting in and out of the turns fast. Changing springs, shocks, rear gears and pan hard bar setting, among other things, a fast-paced process of trial and error begins. Throughout qualifying, team members keep watch on the competition, seeing who's running fast and how they stack up to the competition.

After qualifying, it's time to change just about everything. Where the qualifying lap has to work during a very short run, the race set-up must be fast over the long haul. As the laps accumulate during a long run, the tires get hotter and hotter. The car must be set up differently to accommodate these long runs.

Saturday. Race practice may take place after qualifying on Friday. Drivers may test each other a little during practice or may hold back, not wanting to let the competition know how fast they are.

The last practice before the race is "happy hour." After the Busch race on Saturday, the Cup teams have one hour (strictly timed) to try to get it right. Happy hour is one of the most critical times for a team. The set-up the car ends happy hour with, is usually the setup it will start the race with. If the teams don't get the lap speeds they need to be competitive during happy hour, or

Load after load of equipment is brought off the hauler. It then becomes the base of operation throughout the weekend.

Cars are carried on a platform in the top of the trailer. This leaves room for tools, spare parts and even a kitchen and lounge.

can't practice because of a mechanical failure, the car will enter the race with an untested set-up. This is never considered an advantage, but races have indeed been won with untested set-ups. After happy hour the cars do not go back on the track until the race.

Sunday. On Sunday morning, the final preparations take place in the garage, and the teams set up the pit areas. At this time, teams make final preparations, checking and rechecking the cars' systems. Every nut and bolt is checked for tightness; all linkages, belts, hoses and other components are inspected to ensure that a small, ordinary part doesn't take the car out of the race. The cars are then pushed out to the starting grid, and after the pre-race festivities, the action finally begins.

After the race, all equipment must be loaded back on the truck and made ready for the trip back to the shop, where on Monday morning it will begin all over again.

Meeting the Press

Throughout the race weekend, drivers are available to both the fans and the press. At the track, the driver has few places to go. Drivers usually have a large RV at the track for themselves and their families. This allows for some family time, which is needed with so many weeks of the year spent on the road.

The rest of the driver's time is spent in the garage. This is where the drivers are usually very visible. Many an autograph has been signed and interview given on the back steps of the car hauler. Press access to the garage area is liberal and interviews are given after practice and qualifying, and before, during and after the race.

Every nook and cranny of the hauler is crammed with equipment.

The Set-Up

Most of the crew chief's (and driver's) weekend is spent making the car handle better or "working on the set-up." The set-up is the combination of engine power, handling ability, braking ability and aerodynamic qualities of the racecar.

The engine set-up is worked out on the dyno before leaving the shop. Both the qualifying and race motors have been custom tuned for the track being raced, set up so that the car will produce power when the driver needs it the most.

Engine power is without a doubt an essential element in making a car go fast—but by far not the only element. In auto racing, three additional areas are important in producing a competitive car: good suspension, good brakes and aerodynamic efficiency.

Suspension

Engine power increases the speed of the car only as long as the suspension can efficiently transfer that power to the track. Additional power does not help if it cannot be controlled. Smooth is fast, and an ill-handling car is not smooth.

Fortunes have been made and lost trying to get 3,600 pounds of metal and rubber around an asphalt circle. Understanding handling is understanding racing itself.

As a neutrally (the same amount of weight on each wheel) sprung car goes straight, the weight is distributed evenly on each tire. As the car turns left, the weight is distributed in the following order. The right front carries the most, then the right rear, the left front, and then the left rear. This distribution of force is countered by the suspension of the car to make the car handle in the turns.

Engine swaps are common. After qualifying the motor is always changed. Others must be available in case of failures during practice.

The better the suspension counters the force, the better the car handles. On a racecar, teams begin by changing the spring pressure on each corner of the car to counter these forces. Other than spring rates, many things can be done to tune a suspension. Shocks, panhard bar adjustments, sway bars and tire pressure are the main adjustments that the teams use. This process of tuning the suspension is an integral part of refining the set-up.

Many complex physical forces are at work on a moving racecar. A racecar's handling ability is ultimately determined by the team's ability to adjust the suspension to counter these forces, and by the driver's ability to find the best line around the track to push the car to its limit, but not over it.

The forces affecting the handling of a racecar vary with the position of the car on the track—whether the car is going down a straightaway or in a turn. In a turn, centrifugal force will try to sling the car outward. Tracks are banked in varying degrees to counter this effect. As a rule, the higher the banking, the faster the cars can go. The 38 degree banking at Bristol allows incredible speeds on one of the smallest tracks. Even though the turns are banked, teams must run stiffer springs on the right side to keep the car from bottoming out.

The suspension set-up for a road course car most closely resembles the suspension set-up on a production car. These are the only Winston Cup cars set up to turn right as well as left at speed, just as production cars do. However, all cars raced on a circle track, be it a half-mile short track or a two-and-a-half-mile superspeedway, are designed to turn well only to the left at speed. It would be impossible to turn a Winston Cup car around and drive it clockwise around the track at anywhere close to the speeds reached going counterclockwise.

A suspension change is always a compromise. As with most things in life, when you get one thing you have

Engines and transmissions are pulled together. Here a new motor is bolted to the tranny getting ready for race practice.

to give up another. The better handling racecar is the one set up closest to the edge of the adjustment compromises.

Oversteer and Understeer

Cars are usually said to be loose, tight or just right. Neil Bonnett once said "loose is when you don't see the wreck and tight is when you do."

Being loose is another word for oversteer, a condition during which the car turns or steers too much. The rear of the car wants to swing out to the right. When this problem develops in a racecar, the driver must compensate, usually by slowing down, both entering and through the turns, to avoid oversteer and having the car spin out.

Being tight, also known as pushing, describes understeer, the tendency for the car to go straight when the front wheels are being turned (to continue to "push" forward). If you have ever hit a patch of ice or wet leaves as you were turning and braking at the same time, you experienced a pushing condition (especially in a front wheel drive car, with all of the weight hung out on the front of the car where it has no business being). The car continues to go forward even though you are turning the wheel. When this develops in a racecar, the driver must slow down, entering and going through the turns to avoid having the car push all the way into the wall.

"Wedge adjustments" can be made to the coil springs on each corner of the suspension to fix these conditions. The upward pressure that the coil spring exerts on the frame is critical to a car's handling ability. Wedge adjustments are made by turning a bolt that runs

EXIDE BATTERIES
CITGO
wood brothers RACING TEAM
Purolator FILTERS
Ford
ARP
STP

Spark plug reading is still a cornerstone of determining how an engine is running.

Quickly up on jack stands a quick spring and shock change is common when working in the set-up during practice.

through the frame rail and is attached to a fixture holding the top of the coil spring. By tightening the bolt, the spring is squeezed tighter increasing the spring pressure or spring rate.

When wedge adjustments are necessary during pit stops, they are usually made on the rear springs. A wrench inserted through the rear window turns the bolt. The front springs cannot be adjusted without opening the hood. Tightening the left rear spring increases the spring rate and puts more pressure on the right front of the car. Likewise, lessening the spring rate on the left rear will take pressure off the right front tire.

This sounds more complicated than it is. If you take a small spring and squeeze it between your thumb and forefinger, the further you squeeze the harder it becomes to continue to squeeze. That is, it takes much less strength to squeeze the first quarter-inch than the last quarter-inch.

Other than wedge other adjustments may be made to affect handling. Spring rubbers—solid rubber bushings—can also be inserted into the spring to "stiffen it

E&A
Budweiser
25
GMAC
QUAKER STATE
Ford

Back and forth from the track to the garage, much of the work is trial and error. A change in the suspension and then a few laps to see how it feels to the driver.

How the weight is distributed is critical to the handling of a racecar. Here a Rick Hendrick-owned Monte Carlo is weighed by the crew. This will also be checked during inspection.

up." The rear spoiler, which dramatically influences how the racecar handles, may be adjusted. More angle means more down force, less angle means less down force. There is a fine line between speed and control on longer tracks. The lower the angle of the spoiler, the less resistance, allowing the car to go faster in the straightaways. On the other hand, the car will not have as much down force on the rear and is much more likely to be loose, and difficult to control in the turns. Too much spoiler and the car will have plenty of down force for the turns, but will suffer on the straights.

A certain amount of air must pass through the front grill to cool the engine. This open grill area creates drag and lift on the front of the car. The bigger the opening, the greater the drag and lift and the lower the speed. Likewise, the smaller the opening, the less the drag and the greater the speed. Teams may tape over some of the grill opening with duct tape, thus reducing the size of the opening and drag and lift. This can only be done as long as sufficient flow to the radiator remains.

The rear spoiler is refined on Jeff Gordon's Chevrolet by crew chief Ray Everham.

Tires

Tires and tire pressures also make up a large part of the set-up. Adjusting tire pressure is a good example of how the smallest of changes can make a dramatic change in a car's handling. On a street car, a couple of pounds of variation in tire pressure will not affect performance and will not be noticeable to the driver. However, on a racecar the handling characteristics of a car can be drastically changed by varying the tire pressure among the four tires. A couple of pounds more or less in a particular tire can fine tune the handling of a racecar. The more pressure in a tire, the stiffer the sidewall of a tire becomes. As with springs and shocks, this sidewall stiffness can be controlled and used to fine tune the set-up.

The alignment of the car will also affect its handling. The alignment is set before the teams leave for the track and usually checked and refined during the weekend to improve tire wear or handling. Contact with the wall or other cars, running over a piece of debris, or running off the track can all result in the alignment being knocked out of its proper setting, causing immediate handling problems. And the alignment is hard to fix without going laps down.

Brakes

On road courses and shorter tracks, having power and a good suspension won't help if the brakes won't slow the car when entering the turn. If a driver has brake problems, he must either slow down using the engine and transmission (which places additional strain on the transmission and the rear end) or he must reduce his speed in the straight so that he won't be carrying as much speed into the turn. Either way, brake problems can quickly turn an otherwise competitive car into an also ran.

Engine tuning continues through out the weekend. Robert Yates is now arguably the Winston Cup king of horsepower. His Ford Thunderbirds are consistent winners on the circuit.

Aerodynamic Flow

Aerodynamic flow is also part of the set-up. Theoretically the only time aerodynamics don't matter is when the car is sitting still. On longer intermediate tracks and superspeedways, the aerodynamic flow—the ability for the car to cut through the air—becomes critical. Teams go to great effort to maximize a car's aerodynamic efficiency, using wind tunnels for testing and learning which small changes to the body improve the speed of cars being run at longer tracks. For instance, the hinges for the hood and deck lid may extend outside the body work on short track and road course cars, but they are recessed on superspeedway cars. The total resistance given by these hinges is roughly equivalent to that of a sewing thimble glued to the hood of the car. But every little bit counts. If a car has body damage, its ability to cut through the air will be lessened, especially if the front facia is damaged. Even minor dents can slow the car down on superspeedways. On short tracks, aerodynamic flow is not as important and many battered racecars have made their way to victory lane, a few with no front body at all.

Different tracks place different demands on a car, and as a result, the team's preparation for each race may be different. A car that is to be run at Talladega (where aerodynamics play such a role and the driver never gets off the throttle) is very different from one that would be run at Martinsville (where the driver is on and off the throttle all day and abuses the brakes diving into the turns). The following are general set-ups for the main four types of tracks run. Keep in mind that each track has a set-up of its own.

The height of the car is measured with a "go/no go" gauge. The lower the car, the less air resistance and the faster a car can go. If the car is too low, it will not be allowed to race.

Superspeedway Set-Up

Springs	Shocks	Tire Pressure
LF 1100	LF: 325-125	LF: 45 pounds
RF 1200	RF: 588-180	RF: 55 pounds
LR 200	LR: 325-125	LR: 45 pounds
RR 225	RR: 520-180	RR: 50 pounds

Swaybars: Front: 1-1/8" Rear: None
Spoiler: 40 Degrees
Body Adjustments: Hood and deck lid hinges are recessed. Maximum attention to aerodynamic flow.
Cooling requirements: No cooling for brakes. Standard cooling for rear end.

Intermediate Track Set-Up

Springs	Shocks	Tire Pressure
LF: 1300	LF: 420-180	LF: 30 pounds
RF: 1700	RF: 480-180	RF: 48 pounds
LR: 350	LR: 325-125	LR: 30 pounds
RR: 375	RR: 325-125	RR: 43 pounds

Swaybars: Front: 1-1/16" Rear: None
Spoiler: 70 Degrees
Body Adjustments: More attention to aerodynamic flow.
Cooling requirements: Minimum cooling for brakes. Standard cooling for rear end.

Even with all the pressures of racing, time must be made for the essentials. Most teams opt for home cooking over a concession stand diet.

Smokin'
Joe's
RACING
Transported By:
FEATHERLITE

A walk out to get a runaway tire.

Short Track Set-Up

Springs	Shocks	Tire Pressure
LF 1100	LF: 325-125	LF: 18 pounds
RF 1200	RF: 380-180	RF: 28 pounds
LR 200	LR: 275-110	LR: 18 pounds
RR 225	RR: 275-110	RR: 28 pounds

Swaybars: Front: 1" Rear: None
Spoiler: 70 Degrees
Body Adjustments: No special adjustments.
Cooling requirements: Maximum cooling for brakes and rear end.

Road Course Set-Up

Springs	Shocks	Tire Pressure
LF 1300	LF: 325-110	LF: 38 pounds
RF 1300	RF: 420-140	RF: 38 pounds
LR 250	LR: 325-110	LR: 36 pounds
RR 250	RR: 420-140	RR: 36 pounds

Swaybars: Front: 1-1/16" Rear: 1/2"
Spoiler: 70 Degrees
Body Adjustments: No special adjustments.
Cooling requirements: Maximum cooling for brakes and rear end and transmission.

Lug nuts are glued to the wheel. The studs on the car are longer than stock, which allows tire changers to slam the wheel on the hub and quickly tighten the lug nuts.

Teams try to come to the track with a set-up close to what they will race with. Sometimes the setup is dead on and the car is fast right off the hauler. Other times the first laps run during practice become a depressing moment for everyone on the team.

Once the desired set-up is found (or time runs out and you're stuck starting the race with the one you've got regardless of how undesirable it is) a team must be ready to change it. A racecar's handling characteristics change during the race. The driver and the crew must work together during pit stops to make adjustments to the set-up that can change the handling of a car.

Line Up and Starting Procedures

The line up is determined by qualifying, which takes place on Friday and Saturday. Friday's qualifying determines the first 25 starting positions. For those who did not qualify during the first round, second round qualifying is held on Saturday. The fastest qualifier during the second round will start in 26th position, the second fastest in 27th, and so on. Drivers do have the option of "standing" on their first day qualifying time, and hoping that it will be good enough to make the field.

Race Strategy

It is difficult, if not impossible, to develop a race strategy before the race. Strategies are most often made during the race, once a team can see how they are running in relation to the rest of the field. Some drivers like to run out front, driving each lap hard and leading whenever possible. Others lay back, always running in the top ten saving the car for the end of the race. At some tracks, such as Michigan, fuel mileage may form strategies. If a car is getting good mileage, and the race continues to run under the green flag, a team may run a bit slower and conserve fuel. By doing this, the team may be able to go without a last pit stop, which might just win a race. Other strategies revolve around pit stops. At longer

Comparing the tire temperature on each corner of the car after a run can help teams understand how the car is handling.

tracks, teams may only change two tires (usually the outside) during a stop. By doing this, they spend less time in the pits and gain track position, passing other cars in the pits. This strategy is especially effective on tracks where passing is very difficult.

Pit Stops

Coordinating the pit stops is another of the crew chief's responsibilities. To be successful, this group must work as a fine tuned machine. During a pit stop seconds count. Two crew members bumping into each other may be the difference between coming out of the pits in first place or tenth place. The work itself is difficult and dangerous.

The typical pitstop consists of filling up with gas and changing four tires. By radio, the driver and crew chief decide when to pit. Once the car comes to a stop, the crew begins to add fuel and jack up the right side of the car to change the right side tires. Once the new right side tires are tightened, the tire changers run around the car and loosen the left side. The jack operator lowers the car and runs around the car and jacks up the left side. The old left side tires are pulled off and the new tires tightened. When the jack operator lowers the car, the driver takes off.

Qualifications for the jack operator are strength, dexterity, and a very keen eye. The person must be quick enough to run around the car and all the other team members to place the jack. The jack operator must also watch both of the tire changers to ensure that the tires are properly changed before the car is dropped. If it is dropped too soon, the resulting delay would be substantial, as the car must be rejacked before the problem can be corrected.

The tire changers must also be quick and very skilled with an air gun. It's not easy to undo five lug nuts, yank a reasonably heavy worn tire off, slam another reasonably heavy tire on, and tighten five lug nuts.

Goodyear is the only supplier of tires. Teams buy the tires at the track and Goodyear mounts and balances them. A weekend's tire bill can be staggering. Teams may use over a dozen sets, at about $1300 a set.

Two people are responsible for the fuel. One is the "gas man," who must be strong and have a keen sense of balance. The physical aspects of the job are demanding. The gas man must climb over the pit wall, carrying the full gas can. Eleven gallons at roughly six pounds each makes for an ungainly 70 pounds or so. A gas man must carry the can high so that the fill nozzle can be immediately connected when he reaches the car. This eliminates any extra time required to lift the can to the car.

The other is the "catch-can man." As the fuel flows into the fuel cell during the fueling process, the air in the fuel cell escapes through a vent hose located at the left rear of the deck lid. As the tank becomes full, fuel will escape up through this vent tube. The catch-can man's job is to insure that the gas escaping from this vent is contained so that it cannot ignite. This position was added after fuel overflow caused a number of fires during pit stops. The catch-can man can also assist the gas man in supporting the fill tank.

Keep in mind that many times while pit stops are happening, the caution is out and everybody else is pitting. Even with the pit road speed limits, pit stops can be scary. Cars are accelerating heavily after pit stops, getting the rear end loose, and decelerating from up to 50 miles per hour, usually skidding the last few feet with the brakes locked. While all of this is going on around them, the crew members have to block it out and concentrate on the job at hand.

94
Ford
94
Motorcraft
BATTERIES
MOOG
SIMPSON
76
ARLO
3M

Victory or Defeat?

CHAPTER 5

So you've spent all of that lottery money, run twelve laps, and what remains of your car is on the trailer. The crew is dejected and you're twelve hundred miles from home. It's the sixth week in a row that you haven't finished a race. The sponsor understands it was a racing incident, but also understands that the exposure for a racecar is strictly limited if it's wrecked and inside a trailer.

Winning a race is often not just having a fast car, but being the fastest car running at the end. Each winner usually has to dodge a bullet or two during the race. Sometimes the bullet can't be dodged and anything from a mild incident, to a full-fledged, "half the cars in the field" pileup will take place. Impact with other cars or the wall can obviously affect a car's set-up. The performance of the damaged car varies, depending on where the damage occurs and on what type of track the race is being run. Dents along the side of the car will not have much of an impact on short tracks and road courses, but may ruin a car's competitiveness on longer tracks.

1985 Winston Cup Champion Bill Elliott dives into the pits for tires and fuel.

A fun day at work. Wrecks at the track mean job security for the team fabricators.

A Stavola Brother's Ford gets a new front end. Many wrecked cars can be repaired, as long as the whole car is not distorted. Many are written off as total loses and some wrecks are even donated to museums.

Assessing the Damage

Some places on the car are more vulnerable than others. Damage to the left front of the car can be fatal, whereas the same damage could be done to the right front and the car could continue racing. The oil cooler is mounted just behind the sheet metal in the left front corner. If the cooler is damaged, the engine will not last. Likewise, damage to the left rear can damage the fuel inlet, hindering refueling during pit stops. If the car is hit broadside against a wheel, the car may be knocked out of alignment. Sometimes a tire blows and sends the car into the wall. There is always the possibility of getting caught up in someone else's wreck. And anything can break. Suspension pieces, rear ends, and transmissions all may fail.

All in the Engine

The motor can be a problem as well. Overheating can be a killer. A number of things can cause a racecar to over-

CITY
Kendall
MOTOR OIL
GOODYEAR
EAGLE

Getting ready to hit the track, a generator provides power to preheat the oil and ensure a full charge to the battery.

heat—internal engine problems, a small leak in a head gasket or a cooling system problem such as a partial or complete blocking of the front grill. Small pieces of rubber, shredded from the soft race tires, often clog the grill. If they get past the grill, they can clog the radiator, reducing its ability to cool the engine. A sandwich wrapper can end a race for a team if it remains pressed against the grill and cuts off the air flow to the radiator and oil cooler.

If the overheating involves an internal engine problem, chances are the team cannot correct it on the spot. All that can be done is to make sure that as much coolant as possible is kept in the cooling system. If the overheating is caused by grill obstructions, the crew can try to clean out the grill during pit stops. However, if the grill or radiator has become clogged with tire rubber, the degree to which it can be cleaned is limited.

When a car has "lost a cylinder," the engine has some type of internal failure, causing it to quit making power in one of its eight cylinders. While such a failure may not be bad enough to completely stop an engine, it is a most serious problem. Obviously, the engine has lost at least one-eighth of its ability to build power, and it is running out of balance, far out of its design range, which may lead to total engine failure.

Another nemesis of the engine builder is "burning a piston." And pre-detonation is the most common cause of piston failure.

The typical modern production engine has a compression ratio of 8.5 to 1. This ratio is calculated by dividing the volume of the cylinder at the bottom of the stroke (the top of the piston at the bottom of the cylinder) by the volume of the cylinder at the top of the stroke

The familiar racing colors of Richard Petty's STP Pontiac. The blue and red 43 has run the circuit for decades and is one of the oldest sponsor/car marriages in history.

(the top of the piston at the top of the cylinder). Winston Cup cars run compression ratios of around 15 to 1.

In a properly functioning engine the mixture of air and fuel in the cylinder is ignited or detonated (near the top of the stroke) by the spark plug. Pre-detonation takes place when the fuel/air mixture is ignited too soon by the pressure of compression, before the piston is at the point of the stroke where ignition of the fuel/air mixture should take place. The piston then continues upward, further compressing the exploding fuel air/mixture and causing further detonations. Then the spark plug fires, re-detonating the whole mess. This series of detonations builds up more heat than a proper, one-time firing at the top of the stroke. As this heat builds, it can burn a hole all the way through the top of the piston causing total engine failure. With Winston Cup engines turning plus or minus 9,000rpm for 500 miles, it is surprising that more engines don't experience catastrophic failure.

A lost cylinder may be the result of a valve train problem. Either a rocker arm, valve spring or valve has broken or otherwise stopped functioning. When a car has lost a cylinder, there is very little a team may do to correct the problem. The driver usually keeps the car on the track, nursing it around and accumulating as many laps as possible for championship points.

The electronic ignition system used in Winston Cup racing provides and controls the spark which fires the engine and can be very temperamental. Because of this high possibility of failure, Winston Cup cars carry two ignition modules, both mounted inside the car, next to the driver. If one fails, the driver can switch to the back-up. If the second unit fails, the team must take a lengthy pit stop to install a new unit.

Drivers can also "blow" an engine. A missed shift can over-rev an engine, causing failure. Or, if a driver pulls in behind another car at 190 miles per hour, the reduced air resistance encountered in drafting can cause a slight increase in the rpm of the engine. If the motor is already red-lined, this may be all it takes to blow the motor. Many things can go wrong with an engine causing it to quit or blow, but in reality, few in Winston Cup racing do.

Yep, overall Winston Cup Racing can be a damned depressing proposition. If you win it's addictive and makes not winning that much harder. Waiting for that first win may take forever, and if you get the first, the wait for the second can be longer. A race team never completely holds their own destiny it their own hands. Finishing well week to week is the product of their effort and the luck of the track. Racing incidents, mechanical failures, and both good and bad luck combine to produce their destiny. A team can make much of their own luck, but they will never make it all.

The pit stall is set up on raceday morning. A full complement of tools, parts, fuel and tires will be taken to the pits.

Top Right
The tool cart equipment ranges from simple tools to satellite dish, television and computers.

Bottom Right
Air for the wrenches used during the pit stops is supplied from cans housed in the bottom of the pit cart.

RCA
RCA
STP

Pit stop equipment is checked and rechecked. Equipment failure during a pit stop can mean losing a race that could have been won.

The smallest detail can help win a race. In case a lug nut is dropped, another is handy.

The Richard Childress Racing pit crew performs another flawless pit stop.

Fuel is the responsibility of Unocal. The racing fuel is given out two cans at a time. A crew member will shuttle back and forth during the race to get more.

Slight damage at a short track or road course isn't much of a worry, but will kill a chance of a win on longer tracks where aerodynamics are so critical.

As terrible as they look, most drivers walk away from most accidents and are usually racing the next week. Dale Earnhardt qualified and started the race a week after this wreck at Talladega.

A 200 mile per hour superspeedway "nose job."

Although seriously damaged, some cars will return to the track to accumulate points.

Some cars are so damaged, that the team has no choice but to call it a day.

Even the boss works at Robert Yates Racing. The cars are pushed though inspection and onto the starting grid on raceday morning.

Winston Cup Officials watch the pit stops checking for rules violations such as running over air hoses or too many men over the wall. They also check safety items, such as proper catch can use and that all lug nuts are in place and secure.

Next Page
NASCAR Officials check carburetors and other engine components.

Series
NASCAR Winston Cup Series
Kodak FILM
Delco BATTERY
AC
76
4

Goodwrench
Service
RCR
3
NEW HOLLAND

Bud
SOR OF THE 1996 U.S. OLYMPIC TEAM
USA
GOODYEAR
GOODYEAR

Any Car that's going to race must fit the NASCAR templates. These go from front to back over the center of the car, however there are templates for many areas on the body.

CHEVROLET
AC
Skittles
NASCAR RACE CAR
NASCAR Winston Cup
True Value
Western Auto
BUSCH BEER Pole Award Winner
AP
DU PONT AUTOMOTIVE FINISHES
Gatorade
CLEVITE 77 ENGINE BEARINGS
HURST SHIFTERS
Goody's HEADACHE POWDERS
Holley CARBS
Stant RADIATOR PRESSURE CAPS
RCA
3M
Bowman
GOODYEAR
EAGLE
plasti-kote
24

The crew chief most often accompanies the car through inspection. Here Ray Everham walks Jeff Gordon's Chevy Monte Carlo through inspection.

Inspection & Rules

True story (well I heard it on a Paul Harvey news report) about a politician who was running fourth out of four in a particular district on election day. His solution was buying enough beer, whiskey and rum, roughly a quart and a half for each voter in this district. He became instantly popular, won the election and became the father of our country, George Washington. He cheated yes but since he's G.W. . . we don't hold it against him.

Cheating on the Winston Cup circuit seems to be looked on in the same light. Cars are built to specific regulations established by NASCAR. Each year the teams are furnished with a rule book specifying how the car will be built and what parts and materials are legal and which ones aren't. When you start adding up all of the pieces in a car, all of the positions that they must be located, all of the complex angles and curves of the bodies, it becomes very difficult to write a rule book that covers everything. The teams must interpret the rules and they interpret them in different ways since each team's cars have small differences. Some teams interpret them so differently that NASCAR officials may hammer them for tens of thousands of dollars after they go through inspection.

There are different kind of rules infractions. Some may be an accidents or innocent misunderstanding of the rule and result in little or no fine. However, some infractions are pretty much premeditated, really sneaky and really illegal and more often than not result in heavy fines. Some of the current fines have been as high as $50,000 or more. From oversized engines to body leveling devices, the NASCAR officials have seen it all and continue to see more every year.

All competing cars are inspected before each race, and may be inspected at any time during and after the race. Due to the fact that all racecars will be somewhat different, inspection procedures take place not only to catch premeditated cheating, but also to ensure maximum competitiveness. Racecars are built by different people, in different places, at different times, with parts from different suppliers, all using the same rules.

These rules can be interpreted in a variety of ways. Indeed, just as teams must constantly look for an edge in their engine and chassis, they must constantly look for edges in the rule book, finding different ways to go faster while staying within NASCAR's rule specifications. In building the cars, teams interpret the rules in search of slight advantages that might provide the edge on the track. With the number of cars competing and the number of parts on a Winston Cup car, inspecting for violations is a difficult job for the officials. It is impossible for the rule makers to think of everything, but the teams usually will. Inspection procedures ensure that the "spirit" of the rules is observed, again keeping the playing field as level as possible.

At the track, the inspection area is used by all the teams before and during practice runs to ensure that changes made in the set-up don't take the car out of tolerance. These "self-inspections" ensure that the set-up being tested is legal and prevents any embarrassing moments during formal inspections. Cars may be sealed or impounded, and fines levied if rule violations are found.

Under the watchful eye of inspection officials, Richard Childress Racing's crew make the carb and restricter plate available for viewing.

Air dam height and rear spoiler angle are closely monitored by NASCAR officials.

Appendix A

Top 40 200-Plus Qualifiers

Drivers	Speed (mph)	Race
Bill Elliott	212.809	1987 Winston 500
Bill Elliott	212.229	1986 Winston 500
Bobby Allison	211.797	1987 Winston 500
Davey Allison	210.61	1987 Winston 500
Darrell Waltrip	210.471	1987 Winston 500
Bill Elliott	210.364	1987 Daytona 500
Dale Earnhardt	210.36	1987 Winston 500
Kyle Petty	210.346	1987 Winston 500
Sterling Marlin	210.194	1987 Winston 500
Terry Labonte	210.101	1987 Winston 500
Phil Parsons (tie)	209.963	1987 Winston 400
Lake Speed (tie)	209.963	1987 Winston 500
Geoff Bodine	209.71	1987 Winston 500
Buddy Baker	209.701	1987 Winston 500
Bill Elliott	209.398	1985 Winston 500
Bobby Allison	209.274	1986 Winston 500
Davey Allison	209.084	1987 Daytona 500
Bill Elliott	209.005	1986 Talladega 500
Ron Bouchard	208.91	1987 Winston 500
Rusty Wallace	208.251	1987 Winston 500
Ken Schrader	208.227	1987 Daytona 500
Geoff Bodine	208.169	1986 Winston 500
Ken Schrader	208.16	1987 Winston 500
Bobby Hillin Jr.	208.142	1987 Winston 500
Ricky Rudd	208.138	1987 Winston 500
Cale Yarborough (tie)	208.092	1986 Winston 500
Cale Yarborough (tie)	208.092	1987 Winston 500
Dale Earnhardt	208.052	1986 Talladega 500
Morgan Shepherd	207.831	1987 Winston 500
Bobby Allison	207.795	1987 Daytona 500
Sterling Marlin	207.776	1986 Winston 500
Benny Parsons	207.659	1987 Winston 500
Bill Elliott	207.578	1985 Talladega 500
Tim Richmond	207.538	1986 Talladega 500
Benny Parsons (tie)	207.403	1986 Talladega 500
Neil Bonnett (tie)	207.403	1987 Winston 500
Morgan Shepherd	207.389	1986 Winston 500
Greg Sacks	207.246	1987 Winston 500
Sterling Marlin	207.192	1986 Talladega 500
Buddy Baker	207.151	1986 Winston 500

•58 Drivers have run 200 or better during their Winston Cup careers. Cale Yarborough has topped 200 fifteen times to lead this list.

First Time Winners Winston Cup Series

Year	Driver
1996	Bobby Hamilton
1995	Bobby Labonte, Ward Burton
1994	Jimmy Spencer, Jeff Gordon
1993	None
1992	None
1991	Dale Jarrett
1990	Derrike Cope, Brett Bodine, Ernie Irvan
1989	Mark Martin
1988	Lake Speed, Phil Parsons, Ken Schrader, Alan Kulwicki
1987	Davey Allison
1986	Kyle Petty, Rusty Wallace, Bobby Hilin Jr.
1985	Greg Sacks
1984	Geoff Bodine
1983	Ricky Rudd, Bill Elliott
1982	Harry Gant, Tim Richmond
1981	Morgan Shepherd Jody Ridley, Ron Bouchard
1980	Terry Labonte
1979	Dale Earnhardt
1978	Lennie Pond
1977	Neil Bonnett
1976	None
1975	Dave Marcis, Darrell Waltrip
1974	Earl Ross
1973	Dick Brooks, Mark Donohue
1972	None

Crown-Jewel Winners

Year	Daytona 500	Winston Select 500	Coca-Cola 600	Southern 500
1996	Dale Jarrett	Sterling Marlin	Dale Jarrett	Jeff Gordon
1995	Sterling Marlin	Mark Martin	Bobby Labonte	Jeff Gordon
1994	Sterling Marlin	Dale Earnhardt	Jeff Gordon	Bill Elliott
1993	Dale Jarrett	Ernie Irvan	Dale Earnhardt	Mark Martin
1992	Davey Allison	Davey Allison	Dale Earnhardt	Darrell Waltrip
1991	Ernie Irvan	Harry Gant	Davey Allison	Harry Gant
1990	Derrike Cope	Dale Earnhardt	Rusty Wallace	Dale Earnhardt
1989	Darrell Waltrip	Davey Allison	Darrell Waltrip	Dale Earnhardt
1988	Bobby Allison	Benny Parsons	Darrell Waltrip	Bill Elliott
1987	Bill Elliott	Davey Allison	Kyle Petty	Dale Earnhardt
1986	Geoff Bodine	Bobby Allison	Dale Earnhardt	Tim Richmond
1985	Bill Elliott	Bill Elliott	Darrell Waltrip	Bill Elliott(a)
1984	Cale Yarborough	Cale Yarborough	Bobby Allison	Harry Gant
1983	Cale Yarborough	Richard Petty	Neil Bonnett	Bobby Allison
1982	Bobby Allison	Darrell Waltrip	Neil Bonnett	Cale Yarborough
1981	Richard Petty	Bobby Allison	Bobby Allison	Neil Bonnett
1980	Buddy Baker	Buddy Baker	Benny Parsons	Terry Labonte
1979	Richard Petty	Bobby Allison	Darrell Waltrip	David Pearson
1978	Bobby Allison	Cale Yarborough	Darrell Waltrip	Cale Yarborough
1977	Cale Yarborough	Darrell Waltrip	Richard Petty	David Pearson
1976	David Pearson	Buddy Baker	David Pearson	David Pearson(b)
1975	Benny Parsons	Buddy Baker	Richard Petty	Bobby Allison
1974	Richard Petty	David Pearson	David Pearson	Cale Yarborough
1973	Richard Petty	David Pearson	Buddy Baker	Cale Yarborough
1972	A.J. Foyt	David Pearson	Buddy Baker	Bobby Allison
1971	Richard Petty	Donnie Allison	Bobby Allison	Bobby Allison
1970	Pete Hamilton	Peter Hamilton	Donnie Allison	Buddy Baker
1969	LeeRoy Yarborough	n/a	LeeRoy Yarborough	LeeRoy Yarborough(c)

(a) Bill Elliott became the first driver to win the Winston Million. The $1 million from Winston goes to any driver who wins three of the four crown jewels of the NASCAR Winston Cup Circuit. (Initiated in 1985)

(b) David Pearson won three of the Big Four races.

(c) LeeRoy Yarborough won the NASCAR Triple Crown.

n/a - There was no Winston 500 that year as work was still being done on the Alabama International Motor Speedway.

Winston Cup Rookies of the Year
1958-1996

Year	Driver	Races	Wins	Poles	Top 5	Top 10	Winnings
1996	Johnny Benson	30	0	0	1	6	$893,888
1995	Ricky Craven	31	0	0	0	4	$597,054
1994	Jeff Burton	30	0	0	2	3	$594,700
1993	Jeff Gordon	30	0	1	7	11	$765,168 (a)
1992	Jimmy Hensley	22	0	0	0	4	$247,660
1991	Bobby Hamilton	28	0	0	0	4	$259,105
1990	Rob Moroso	25	0	0	0	1	$162,002
1989	Dick Trickle	28	0	0	6	9	$343,728
1988	Ken Bouchard	24	0	0	0	1	$109,410
1987	Davey Allison	22	2	5	9	10	$361,080
1986	Alan Kulwicki	23	0	0	1	4	$94,450 (b)
1985	Ken Schrader	28	0	0	0	3	$211,523
1984	Rusty Wallace	30	0	0	2	4	$195,927 (c)
1983	Sterling Marlin	30	0	0	0	1	$143,564
1982	Geoff Bodine	25	0	2	4	10	$258,500
1981	Ron Bouchard	22	1	1	5	12	$152,855
1980	Jody Ridley	31	0	0	2	18	$196,617
1979	Dale Earnhardt	27	1	4	11	17	$264,088 (d)
1978	Ronnie Thomas	27	0	0	0	2	$73,037
1977	Ricky Rudd	25	0	0	1	10	$68,448
1976	Skip Manning	27	0	0	0	4	$55,820
1975	Bruce Hill	26	0	0	3	11	$58,138
1974	Earl Ross	21	1	0	5	10	$64,830
1973	Lennie Pond	23	0	0	1	9	$25,155
1972	Larry Smith	23	0	0	0	7	$24,215
1971	Walter Ballard	41	0	0	3	11	$25,598
1970	Bill Dennis	25	0	0	0	5	$15,670
1969	Dick Brooks	28	0	0	3	12	$27,532
1968	Pete Hamilton	16	0	0	3	6	$8,239
1967	Donnie Allison	20	0	0	4	7	$16,440
1966	James Hylton	41	0	1	20	32	$29,575
1965	Sam McQuagg	15	0	0	2	5	$10,555
1964	Doug Cooper	39	0	0	4	11	$10,445
1963	Billy Wade	22	0	0	4	11	$8,710
1962	Tom Cox	40	0	0	12	20	$8,980
1961	Woody Wilson	5	0	0	0	1	$2,625
1960	David Pearson	22	0	1	3	7	$5,030 (e)
1959	Richard Petty	22	0	0	6	9	$7,630 (f)
1958	Shorty Rollins	21	1	0	10	17	$8,515

(a) Jeff Gordon won the 1995 Championship.
(b) Alan Kulwicki won the 1992 Championship.
(c) Rusty Wallace won the 1984 Championship.
(d) Dale Earnhardt won the 1980, 1986, 1987, 1990, 1991, 1993 and 1994 Winston Cup Championships.
(e) David Pearson won the 1966, 1968, and 1969 championships.
(f) Richard Petty won the 1964, 1967, 1971, 1972, 1974, 1975 and 1979 championships.

Winston Cup Champions and Runners-Up

Year	Champion	Runner Up	Spread
1996	Terry Labonte	Jeff Gordon	37
1995	Jeff Gordon	Dale Earnhardt	34
1994	Dale Earnhardt	Mark Martin	444
1993	Dale Earnhardt	Rusty Wallace	80
1992	Alan Kulwicki	Ricky Rudd	10
1991	Dale Earnhardt	Dale Earnhardt	195
1990	Dale Earnhardt	Mark Martin	26
1989	Rusty Wallace	Dale Earnhardt	12
1988	Bill Elliott	Rusty Wallace	24
1987	Dale Earnhardt	Bill Elliott	489
1986	Dale Earnhardt	Darrell Waltrip	288
1985	Darrell Waltrip	Bill Elliott	101
1984	Terry Labonte	Harry Gant	65
1983	Bobby Allison	Darrell Waltrip	47
1982	Darrell Waltrip	Bobby Allison	72
1981	Darrell Waltrip	Bobby Allison	53
1980	Dale Earnhardt	Cale Yarborough	19
1979	Richard Petty	Darrell Waltrip	11
1978	Cale Yarborough	Bobby Allison	474
1977	Cale Yarborough	Richard Petty	386
1976	Cale Yarborough	Richard Petty	195
1975	Richard Petty	Dave Marcis	722
1974	Richard Petty	Cale Yarborough	567.45
1973	Benny Parsons	Cale Yarborough	67.15
1972	Richard Petty	Bobby Allison	127.90

Multiple Winston Cup Champions

Driver	Years
Dale Earnhardt	1994, 1993, 1991, 1990, 1987, 1986, 1980
Richard Petty	1979, 1975, 1974, 1972, 1971, 1967, 1964
Darrell Waltrip	1985, 1982, 1981
Cale Yarborough	1978, 1977, 1976
David Pearson	1969, 1968, 1966
Lee Petty	1959, 1958, 1954
Terry Labonte	1996, 1984
Ned Jarrett	1965, 1961
Joe Weatherly	1963, 1982
Buck Baker	1957, 1956
Tim Flock	1955, 1952
Herb Thomas	1953, 1951

Top 10 Closest Winston Cup Championships

Year	Champion	Runner Up	Point Margin
1992	Alan Kulwicki	Bill Elliott	10
1979	Richard Petty	Darrell Waltrip	11
1989	Rusty Wallace	Dale Earnhardt	12
1980	Dale Earnhardt	Cale Yarborough	19
1988	Bill Elliott	Rusty Wallace	24
1990	Dale Earnhardt	Mark Martin	26
1995	Jeff Gordon	Dale Earnhardt	34
1996	Terry Labonte	Jeff Gordon	37
1983	Bobby Allison	Darrell Waltrip	47
1981	Darrell Waltrip	Bobby Allison	53

NASCAR Winston Cup Champions 1949-1996

Year	Number	Driver	Owner	Car	Wins	Poles	Winnings
1996	5	Terry Labonte	Rick Hendrick	Chevrolet	2	4	$3,500,000 (est.)
1995	24	Jeff Gordon	Rick Hendrick	Chevrolet	7	9	$4,300,000
1994	3	Dale Earnhardt	Richard Childress	Chevrolet	4	2	$3,300,733
1993	3	Dale Earnhardt	Richard Childress	Chevrolet	6	2	$3,353,789
1992	7	Alan Kulwicki	Alan Kulwicki	Ford	2	6	$2,322,561
1991	3	Dale Earnhardt	Richard Childress	Chevrolet	4	0	$2,396,685
1990	3	Dale Earnhardt	Richard Childress	Chevrolet	9	4	$3,083,056
1989	27	Rusty Wallace	Baymond Beadle	Pontiac	6	4	$2,247,950
1988	9	Bill Elliott	Harry Meling	Ford	6	6	$1,574,639
1987	3	Dale Earnhardt	Richard Childress	Chevrolet	11	1	$2,099,243
1986	3	Dale Earnhardt	Richard Childress	Chevrolet	5	1	$1,783,880
1985	11	Darrell Waltrip	Junior Johnson	Chevrolet	3	4	$1,318,735
1984	44	Terry Labonte	Billy Hagen	Chevrolet	2	2	$713,010
1983	22	Bobby Allison	Bill Gardner	Buick	6	0	$828,355
1982	11	Darrell Waltrip	Junior Johnson	Buick	12	7	$873,118
1981	11	Darrell Waltrip	Junior Johnson	Buick	12	11	$693,342
1980	2	Dale Earnhardt	Ros Ostenlund	Chevrolet	5	0	$588,926
1979	43	Richard Petty	Petty Ent.	Chevrolet	5	1	$531,292
1978	11	Cale Yarborough	Junior Johnson	Oldsmobile	10	8	$530,751
1977	11	Cale Yarborough	Junior Johnson	Chevrolet	9	3	$477,499
1976	11	Cale Yarborough	Junior Johnson	Chevrolet	9	2	$387,173
1975	43	Richard Petty	Petty Ent.	Dodge	13	3	$378,865
1974	43	Richard Petty	Petty Ent.	Dodge	10	7	$299,175
1973	72	Benny Parsons	L.G. DeWitt	Chevrolet	1	0	$114,345
1972	43	Richard Petty	Petty Ent.	Plymouth	8	3	$227,015
1971	43	Richard Petty	Petty Ent.	Plymouth	21	9	$309,225
1970	71	Bobby Isaac	Nord Krauskopf	Dodge	11	13	$121,470
1969	17	David Pearson	Holman-Moody	Ford	11	14	$183,700
1968	17	David Pearson	Holman-Moody	Ford	16	12	$118,842
1967	43	Richard Petty	Petty Ent.	Plymouth	27	18	$130,275
1966	6	David Pearson	Cotton Owens	Dodge	14	7	$59,205
1965	11	Ned Jarrett	Bondy Long	Ford	13	9	$77,966
1964	43	Richard Petty	Petty Ent.	Plymouth	9	8	$98,810
1963	8	Joe Weatherly	—	Mercury	3	6	$58,110
1962	8	Joe Weatherly	Bud Moore	Pontiac	9	6	$56,110
1961	11	Ned Jarrett	W.G. Holloway, Jr.	Chevrolet	1	4	$27,285
1960	4	Rex White	White-Clements	Chevrolet	6	3	$45,260
1959	42	Lee Petty	Petty Ent.	Plymouth	10	2	$45,570
1958	42	Lee Petty	Petty Ent.	Oldsmobile	7	4	$20,600
1957	87	Buck Baker	Buck Baker	Chevrolet	10	5	$24,712
1956	300B	Buck Baker	Carl Kiekhaefer	Chrysler	14	12	$29,790
1955	300	Tim Flock	Carl Kiekhaefer	Chrysler	18	19	$33,750
1954	42	Lee Petty	—	Chrysler	7	3	$26,706
1953	92	Herb Thomas	Herb Thomas	Hudson	11	10	$27,300
1952	91	Tim Flock	Ted Chester	Hudson	8	4	$20,210
1951	92	Herb Thomas	Herb Thomas	Hudson	7	4	$18,200
1950	60	Bill Rexford	Julian Buesink	Oldsmobile	1	0	$6,175
1949	22	Red Byron	Raymond Parks	Oldsmobile	2	1	$5,800

Aerodynamic flow - How efficiently a racecar moves through the air. The smoother the body, the more efficiently it moves through the air and the faster it goes. Teams go to great effort to maximize a car's aerodynamic efficiency, using wind tunnels for testing and learning which small changes to the body improve the speed of cars being run at longer, faster tracks.

Brake Fade - A condiition when the brake rotors and pads become so hot that they transfer enough heat to the caliper to boil the brake fluid in the caliper. Boiling occurs when the rotor temperature goes over about 1100 degrees F. When the fluid boils, air is released into the brake lines, causing the pedal to go to the floor when pressed.

Camber - The angle of the top of the fire and the bottom of the tire relative to the vertical centerline of the tire.

Caster - The angle between the ball joints and the vertical centerline of the tire.

Dyno - A machine used to measure the amount of power an engine produces. The engine is hooked up and run in the shop and tested before going into the car.

Inspection - Mandatory NASCAR procedures before, during and after practice, qualifying and the race. Due to the fact that all race cars will be somewhat different, inspection procedures take place not only to catch premeditated cheating, but also to ensure maximum competitiveness. Inspection procedures ensure that the "spirit" of the rules is observed, again keeping the playing field as level as possible.

Oversteer - (Also known as being loose) Oversteer is a condition during which the car turns or steer too much. The rear of the car wants to swing out to the right. When this problem develops in a race car, the driver must compensate, usually by slowing down, both entering and through the turns, to avoid oversteer and having the car spin out.

Rear Spoiler - An Aluminum piece mounted on and extending the full width of the back of the rear deck lid. The spoiler grealy influences how the racecar handles. As air passes over the decklid on the car, it hits the spoiler. The higher the angle, the more resistance the air meets and the more down force is created.

Restricter Plate - A metal plate mounted between the carburetor and intake manifold to reduce air to the engine and thus reduce horsepower slowing the speeds down. Restrictor plates are only used at Daytona and Talladega.

Roof Flaps - Safety devices recently introduced into Stockcar racing. The flaps are recessed into the roof and activate when the car spins. Roof flaps are positioned so that air catches them and keeps the car from becoming airborne.

Set-up - The set-up is a combination of engine power, handling ability, braking ability and aerodynamic qualities that determine how a race car handles. Set-ups vary greatly from track to track.

Spring Rate - The measurement of the amount of pressure in a particular coil spring. Springs of different rates are put on each corner of the car to refine the handling on a particular track.

Stagger - An adjustment made by using different sizes of tires on the car at the same time. By putting tires on the outside of the car that have a slightly larger diameter than the tires on the inside of the car, it turns more efficiently on circular tracks.

Toe - The angle of the front of the tire and the rear of the tire relative to the centerline of the car.

Understeer - (Also known as pushing, or the car being tight) Understeer is the tendency for the car to go straight when the front wheels are being turned (continue to "push" forward). When this develops in a racecar, the driver must slow down entering and going through the turns to avoid having the car push all the way into the wall.

Wedge - A name used to describe adjustments made to the coil springs to fine tune the suspension set-up. The spring rate can be increased or decreased by wedge adjustments. Wedge adjustments can be made on each corner of the suspension; however, only wedge adjustments to the rear can be made without opening the hood.

Index